P9-BBP-109

RPM

MOTORCYCLES

The Ins and Outs of *Superbikes, Choppers, and Other Motorcycles*

By Jeff C. Young

WITHDRAWN

Consultant:
Dan Smith
Resource Development Director
The AMA's Motorcycle Hall of Fame Museum
Pickerington, Ohio

Fitchburg Public Library
5530 Lacy Road
Fitchburg, WI 53711

Capstone press®

Mankato, Minnesota

Velocity is published by Capstone Press,
151 Good Counsel Drive, P.O. Box 669, Mankato, Minnesota 56002.
www.capstonepub.com

Copyright © 2010 by Capstone Press, a Capstone imprint. All rights reserved.
No part of this publication may be reproduced in whole or in part, or stored in a retrieval system, or
transmitted in any form or by any means, electronic, mechanical, photocopying, recording, or otherwise,
without written permission of the publisher. For information regarding permission, write to Capstone Press,
151 Good Counsel Drive, P.O. Box 669, Dept. R, Mankato, Minnesota 56002.
Printed in the United States of America in Stevens Point, Wisconsin.

032010
005737R

Books published by Capstone Press are manufactured with paper containing at least
10 percent post-consumer waste.

Library of Congress Cataloging-in-Publication Data
Young, Jeff C., 1948–
    Motorcycles : the ins and outs of superbikes, choppers, and other motorcycles / by Jeff
C. Young.
      p. cm. — (Velocity — RPM)
    Includes bibliographical references and index.
    Summary: "Describes the details of different types of motorcycles, including superbikes, choppers,
cruisers, touring motorcycles, and dirt bikes" — Provided by publisher.
    ISBN 978-1-4296-3431-1 (library binding)
    ISBN 978-1-4290-4887-5 (paperback)
    1. Motorcycles — Juvenile literature. I. Title. II. Series.
TL440.15.Y679 2010
629.227'5 — dc22   2009003677

Editorial Credits

Carrie Braulick Sheely, editor; Heidi Thompson, designer; Jo Miller, media researcher

Photo Credits

123RF/Andriy Rovenko, 33; AP Images/Douglas C. Pizac, 45; BigStockPhoto.com/geom, 7 (bottom);
BigStockPhoto.com/johndavidka, 4; Capstone Press/Karon Dubke, 6 (all), 8–9, 10–11, 14 (both), 15
(both), 23 (all), 29, 34–35, 36 (both), 37, 39 (bottom), 40–41, 41 (top); Corbis/Bo Bridges, 20–21;
Courtesy of American Honda Motor Co., Inc., 38, 39 (top); fotolia/Milkhail (Kyon) Maklakov, 16–17;
Getty Images Inc./Hulton Archive/Topical Press Agency, 12; Getty Images Inc./Roger Viollet Collection,
5 (bottom); iStockphoto/Dan Barnes, 30; iStockphoto/Dan Knopp, 44–45; iStockphoto/djjohn, 31;
Newscom, 13 (top); Newscom/UPI Photo/Aaron Kehoe, 18–19; Newscom/WENN/Rachel Worth, 28
(top); Shutterstock/afaizal, 24–25, 26, 28 (bottom); Shutterstock/Dole, 7 (middle); Shutterstock/Henk
Bentlage, 42; Shutterstock/Ljupco Smokovski, 32; Shutterstock/maccat, cover; Shutterstock/Margo
Harrison, 7 (top), 43; Shutterstock/Tracey Stearns, 13 (bottom); Wikimedia, 5 (top)

Design Elements

Shutterstock/Betacam-SP; Gordan; High Leg Studio; Nicemonkey

The publisher does not endorse products whose logos may appear in images in this book.

The author dedicates this book to his biker buddy, John Westby.

TABLE OF CONTENTS

THRILLS ON TWO WHEELS

Anyone who has ridden a motorcycle can tell you that there's nothing quite like it. You settle into the seat and start up a purring engine. With a twist of the throttle grip, you're on your way. Whether you're on a dirt path or a curving highway, you can expect an exciting ride.

German inventor Gottlieb Daimler was the first person to build a motorcycle powered by a gasoline engine. In 1885, he mounted the engine onto a wooden two-wheeled vehicle that was similar to a bicycle. Gottlieb's son rode 6 miles (9.7 kilometers) through the countryside before heading home.

Gottlieb's idea took off almost instantly. European and American motorcycle manufacturers battled head-to-head to build the best bikes. They experimented with more powerful engines, stronger chassis, and motorcycles that were easier to control.

Today, millions of people worldwide own motorcycles. They use them for both transportation and recreation. From riders who have a desire to dazzle to those with a need for speed, there's a motorcycle to suit them.

Types of motorcycles often have certain clothing styles and gear associated with them. The riders below are ready to start their engines. Which motorcycles would you pair them with?

A

B

C

dirt bike

sport bike

cruiser

Answers: Rider A & the cruiser; Rider B & the sport bike; Rider C & the dirt bike

CRUISERS

Say the word "motorcycle," and most people think of a cruiser. Most cruisers have powerful engines of 650 cubic centimeters (ccs) or more. The most common cruiser engine is the two-cylinder V-twin model. It's called a V-twin because the two cylinders form a "V" shape. But an almost endless variety of engine options are available. A cruiser can have a three-, four-, or even an eight-cylinder engine.

Harley-Davidson is one of the best-known cruiser manufacturers. Loyal Harley owners claim that it's the best motorcycle ever made. To them, saying that a Harley is just a motorcycle would be like saying that a Rolls-Royce is just a car!

The Harley is famous for its classic look. But it's equally famous for its sound. In a Harley engine, both pistons connect to one crankpin. Most other motorcycle engines have a crankpin for each piston. The Harley's engine design keeps the pistons from firing at even intervals. This uneven firing gives the Harley the rumble everyone knows and loves.

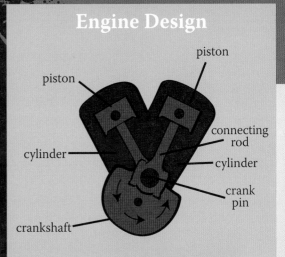

Engine Design

piston

piston

connecting rod

cylinder

cylinder

crank pin

crankshaft

Most people agree that Harley-Davidson's FX Super Glide was the company's first "cruiser." The 1971 Super Glide combined a powerful 1,213-cc engine with the front wheel and forks of the Sportster model. From this basic design, Harley made similar cruisers that took the motorcycle world by storm.

Honda VTX1300C

Seat: A cruiser's seats are designed to make the rider sit in an upright or a slightly forward position.

Fuel Injection: Modern cruisers are equipped with fuel-injected engines. These engines start quicker and more easily than carbureted engines do.

Frame: Cruisers have a long chassis. The frame is usually made of steel tubing. Most of the frame's weight is toward the back.

For several years, Harley dominated the new cruiser market. But in the late 1970s, Japanese manufacturers like Honda, Kawasaki, Suzuki, and Yamaha shipped their cruisers to the United States. Today, both U.S. and foreign cruisers have a huge fan base.

Handlebars: A cruiser's handlebars are usually positioned so that the rider's hands are chest-high.

Front Forks: Cruisers have short front forks that are set close to the frame.

Chrome: Super-shiny chrome parts help the bike attract attention wherever it goes.

THE WRECKING CREW

Harley's racing crew was nicknamed the "Wrecking Crew" because they wrecked the other teams' chances of winning. After one 300-mile (483-kilometer) race in 1915, Harley riders took six of the first seven places. Today, Harley-Davidson sponsors racing teams in drag races and flat track races.

Harley-Davidson racer Freddie Dixon was nicknamed "Flying Freddie." In 1923, he sped around tracks on a Harley with a new engine design. This design featured four valves per cylinder, which helped the engine produce more power.

Who would think about jumping a motorcycle across a canyon or over a stack of 50 cars? Motorcycle daredevil Robert Knievel, known as "Evel Knievel," didn't just consider these feats — he tried them. Knievel thrilled crowds with his hair-raising stunts in the 1970s. Many of these stunts featured his beloved red, white, and blue Harley-Davidson XR-750.

CRUISING TO STURGIS

Each August, swarms of cruiser riders turn a small town named Sturgis into the largest city in South Dakota. In 2008, more than 400,000 riders cruised into Sturgis. They watched races, attended concerts, and proudly paraded their bikes up and down Main Street.

Year: 2009
Engine type: 2-cylinder V-twin
Engine size: 1,584 ccs
Transmission: 6-speed
Dry weight: 718 lb (326 kg)
Special features: • full front and
                     rear fenders
                   • leather saddle
                     bags

HARLEY-DAVIDSON HERITAGE SOFTAIL CLASSIC

Year: 2003
Engine type: 2-cylinder V-twin
Engine size: 745 ccs
Transmission: 5-speed
Dry weight: 504 lb (229 kg)
Special features: • adjustable rear shocks
                   • low seat height

HONDA SHADOW ACE

Year:	2006
Engine type:	2-cylinder V-twin
Engine size:	1,063 ccs
Transmission:	5-speed
Dry weight:	599 lb (272 kg)
Special features:	• long chrome exhaust pipes
	• throttle position sensor (TPS) provides quick throttle response
	• adjustable rear suspension

V STAR 1100 CLASSIC

KAWASAKI VULCAN 900 CLASSIC

Year:	2008
Engine type:	2-cylinder V-twin
Engine size:	903 ccs
Transmission:	5-speed
Dry weight:	557 lb (253 kg)
Special features:	• custom spoke wheels
	• wide rear tire

15

2

DIRT BIKES

For riders who prefer the rough-and-tumble riding of dirt paths and little-traveled trails, a dirt bike is the obvious choice. Miners, lumberjacks, and park workers use dirt bikes on-the-job. But other riders enjoy testing the limits of their bikes in motocross racing, freestyle competitions, or hill climbs.

Dirt bikes have a plastic front fender that sits high above the front wheel.

Inverted front forks increase strength and reduce weight.

Dirt bike engines are located high on the frame to give the bike more clearance. Engines range in size from 60 to 600 ccs. The 125-cc and 250-cc engines are popular choices for racing. A large air filter keeps dirt from being sucked into the engine. Most dirt bikes have a four- or five-speed transmission.

The chassis of most dirt bikes is made of lightweight aluminum instead of steel. Less weight helps the motorcycle travel faster. Most dirt bikes weigh less than 295 pounds (134 kilograms).

In the rock solid and Superman freestyle tricks, the rider removes his feet from the pegs and kicks his legs backward.

A long seat allows riders to move backward or forward to shift their weight.

The exhaust pipe is placed high on the chassis for more clearance.

The bumps on a dirt bike's tires are known as "knobbies." They give the bike improved traction on mud and gravel.

Most dirt bikes have single-disc front and rear brakes. They provide plenty of stopping power for such lightweight machines.

LET THE DIRT FLY!

Dirt bikes received their name for a reason — they are at home in the dirt. And nowhere is that fact more proven than on a motocross or Supercross track.

Motocross tracks are built outdoors. They are between .5 and 2 miles (.8 and 3.2 kilometers) long. Supercross tracks are built in indoor stadiums. They are about .5 mile (.8 kilometer) long.

First turn: The first turn is narrow and sharp. Only a few riders can get through at once. The rider who is first through has the "holeshot."

Whoop-de-doos: a series of small bumps. They are also called whoops. Whoops are usually no higher than 2 feet (.6 meter).

Double: two jumps that are close together

Motocross and Supercross races are run in different classes. Classes are usually based on the bike's engine size. Races are held over a set time or a certain number of laps.

Triple: three jumps in a row

Starting gate: The gate falls backward toward the riders to keep anyone from moving forward too early.

X GAMES ACTION

In 1993, TV network ESPN decided to create a new international sports competition to attract younger viewers. The first event, called the Extreme Games, was held in 1995. The next year, the name changed to the X Games. Dirt bike events like freestyle were a natural fit for the X Games. In freestyle events, riders fly over a series of jumps. While airborne, they do wild tricks with even wilder names like the candy bar and the coffin.

Best Trick is one of the X Games' most exciting dirt bike events. Riders get only two attempts, or runs, to do their most difficult and exciting freestyle trick.

Best Trick scores go from zero to 100. The higher score from the two runs determines how a rider places. In 2006, Travis Pastrana amazed the audience by landing a double backflip. It was the first one ever landed successfully in a competition.

Best Trick riders are rated on:
- style
- creativity
- trick difficulty

Rider: Travis Pastrana
Year: 2004
Tricks Performed:

First Run: One-Handed 360

Second Run: Superman Seat Grab-Indian Air Backflip (pictured)

Scores: 89.2 and 91.2
Result: Bronze Medal

FOUR-STROKE OR TWO-STROKE?

Today, you'll find dirt bikes with both four-stroke and two-stroke engines. In the future, though, manufacturers may produce only four-strokes to help protect the environment.

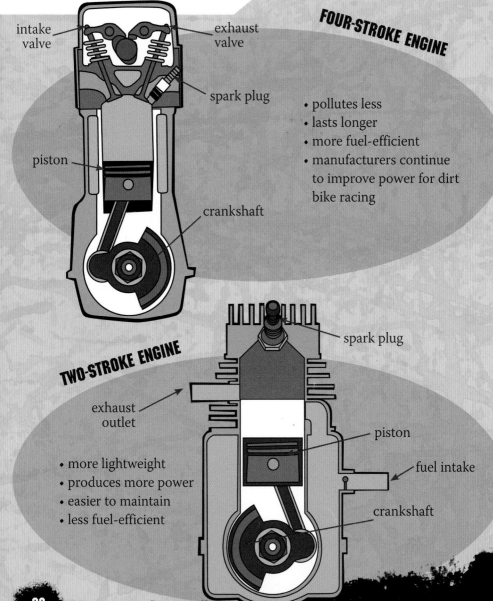

intake valve

exhaust valve

FOUR-STROKE ENGINE

spark plug

piston

crankshaft

- pollutes less
- lasts longer
- more fuel-efficient
- manufacturers continue to improve power for dirt bike racing

spark plug

TWO-STROKE ENGINE

exhaust outlet

piston

fuel intake

crankshaft

- more lightweight
- produces more power
- easier to maintain
- less fuel-efficient

Motocross racing is a dangerous sport. Riders wear full safety gear to reduce their injury risk.

FULL-FACE HELMET: made of strong, lightweight materials such as fiberglass, Kevlar, and carbon fiber. A sun visor increases visibility. Vents help keep the rider cool.

SHIRT AND GLOVES: made of lightweight, breathable material with armor, padding, or reinforcement for extra crash protection

CHEST PROTECTOR: usually made of heavyweight plastic with interior padding for comfort

PANTS: have breathable material and reinforcement at the knees. Spandex panels allow the rider freedom of movement.

BOOTS: Leather boots cover most of a rider's calf. Tread on the bottom keeps a rider's foot from sliding.

SPORT BIKES

For riders with a need for speed, sport bikes are the way to go. Also known as superbikes, crotchrockets, or just "rockets," they're the fastest wheels on the pavement. Forget the plush features. These bikes are made to do one thing — perform.

HANDLEBARS: Low handlebars force riders to lean their upper body forward, which reduces wind resistance.

FAIRINGS: The fairings on sport bikes are aerodynamic. Because the air flows around the bike, the motorcycle can accelerate faster. The fairings are made of plastic or other lightweight materials.

BRAKES: Sport bikes come equipped with very powerful brakes. They have dual-disc brakes in front and a single-disc brake in the rear.

Rider: Anthony West

Racing Team: Kawasaki
Race Type: MotoGP road race
Race: Polini Malaysian Motorcycle Grand Prix

SEAT: A raised seat keeps the rider from sliding backward during times of rapid acceleration.

REAR WHEEL: The rear wheel is wider than the front wheel. The engine drives the rear wheel. Because the tire has more contact with the road, the engine power can provide quick acceleration.

SUPER SLIDING: Racers take corners fast. They put their knee down to judge the lean angle of their bikes. If they lean too far, their bikes will tip. Riders wear knee sliders made of plastic or leather to protect their knees.

Some sport bike riders have the talent and desire to race competitively. The American Motorcyclist Association (AMA) currently sponsors three classes in its road racing circuit. These classes are Superbike, SuperSport, and SportBike. Each class has rules about engine size, fuel type, bike weight, and other specs. There are also rules outlining how much the racing bikes can be changed from the production versions. These rules ensure that the bikes are evenly matched for close and exciting racing. In the Superbike class, riders routinely reach 200 miles (322 kilometers) per hour.

Kawasaki, Suzuki, Yamaha, Honda, and Ducati all sponsor road race teams. Winning championships helps a manufacturer market its bikes.

SPORT BIKE TIRES

In dry weather, racers use tires without tread called slicks. Without tread, the tires stick to the pavement better. But in wet weather, racers use tires with tread. The tread makes a space for the water to escape underneath the tire. Sport bikes used for street riding have tread that is suitable for both dry and wet weather.

The Suzuki GSX1300R, or Hayabusa, is the fastest production sport bike. It has reached speeds of 194 miles (312 kilometers) per hour. At that speed, it takes the rider less than 20 seconds to go 1 mile (1.6 kilometers).

BEHIND THE POWER

Most sport bikes have powerful 600- or 1,000-cc in-line-four engines. In-line-four engines have four cylinders in a row. The engines deliver enough power for the bikes to go from zero to 60 miles (97 kilometers) per hour in about three seconds. Most production sport bikes have a top-end speed of more than 150 miles (241 kilometers) per hour.

ENGINE CYLINDERS

A sport bike's engine runs at high RPMs, or revolutions per minute. A sport bike rider can rev the engine more than a rider on a cruiser. A sport bike accelerates faster than a cruiser as the RPMs rise. It also reaches a higher top speed.

For some riders, road racing has become a family busine brothers in two families — the Bostroms and the Haydens — taken their sibling rivalries to the racetrack.

BEN AND ERIC BOSTROM

NICKY HAYDEN

RIVALRY TIME L

1998 Ben Bostrom wins the AM Superbike Championship. Bostrom clinches the AM Formula Xtreme Champio

2001 Eric Bostrom wins the AN SuperSport Championshi

2002 Nicky Hayden wins the AMA Superbike Championship.

2004 Tommy Hayden wins the AMA SuperSport Championship.

2005 Tommy Hayden clinches the AMA SuperSport for the second year in a row.

2006 Nicky Hayden wins the MotoGP World Championsh

2007 Roger Hayden follows in his older br Tommy's footsteps, winning the AM. SuperSport Championship.

2008 Ben Bostrom wins the AMA SuperSport

It's All in the Family

WHAT'S UNDER ALL THOSE FAIRINGS?

The twin-spar chassis is the most common sport bike frame. Two beams join the steering head to the swing arm pivot bolt in as short of a distance as possible. This strong design reduces bending and twisting of the frame. The engine sits under the frame for good balance.

steering head attaches to top of front fork

swing arm pivot bolt location

Engine is located under the frame.

Using metals like titanium and aluminum for the chassis instead of steel helps keep the bike's weight down. Most sport bikes weigh just 370 to 500 pounds (168 to 227 kilograms). In comparison, mid-weight cruisers often weigh more than 600 pounds (272 kilograms).

In AMA Pro SunTrust Moto-GT races, members of a manufacturer team take turns riding one motorcycle. Series races are 2 hours long, and the final race of the season is 8 hours long. Aprilia, Ducati, Buell, and Suzuki all sponsor teams.

DEFYING GRAVITY

Stunting, or stunt riding, has been around as long as there's been two-wheeled vehicles. The dirt bike is a natural choice for stunt riding because it is powerful yet lightweight. But in recent years, sport bike stunting has become increasingly popular in the United States and Europe.

It's illegal to perform stunts on public roads, so they're performed in parking lots or on short tracks. Stunting competitions have become a regular feature at motorcycle rallies.

The high wheelie is an exciting stunt where the motorcycle is in a nearly vertical position.

An endo, or stoppie, is a reverse wheelie where the rear wheel is off the ground.

Jason Britton is one of the most popular sport bike stunt riders. Britton puts on shows around the world with the other members of Team No Limit.

BREAKING DOWN THE ENDO

The rider keeps his head straight.

The rider keeps his arms stiff.

The rider's body is centered over the bike.

The clutch is pulled in and the front brake is firmly applied. As the rider begins braking, he shifts his weight over the front wheel, and the back wheel pops up.

CHAPTER 4

CHOPPERS

Choppers are more for show than for go. It's true that other motorcycles run faster and are easier to ride. But none of them are quite as eye-catching as a chopper.

The 1960s marked the birth of the chopper as we know it today. Most modern choppers are built from the ground up. Highly successful chopper companies exist all over the United States, just waiting to make one rider's dream a reality.

Who made the first chopper or when it was built isn't known for sure. They became especially popular in the late 1940s. These bikes were production motorcycles that had been stripped of excess weight. Riders chopped off parts such as fenders, mufflers, and chain guards. Some motorcycle clubs modified their choppers by adding taller handlebars. These were a forerunner of a style of handlebars known as "apehangers." Many modern choppers still have this handlebar style.

Orange County Choppers, based in New York, helped rev chopper mania into high gear. Through its TV show, *American Chopper*, people can watch some of the most unique — and expensive — choppers being made from scratch.

A teardrop-shaped gas tank is a common feature on choppers. The tank often has multi-color designs painted on it.

Custom parts, such as this air filter, make a chopper stand out in a crowd.

The seat often has hand-stitched designs in it.

Choppers have low ground clearance.

A chopper's back wheel is often much wider than the front wheel.

On some choppers, the foot controls are closer to the front of the bike than they are on cruisers. The adjustment allows the rider to enjoy a more relaxed riding position.

34

Perhaps the most noticeable feature of a chopper is the extra-long front forks. They make the bike easier to ride when you're moving in a straight line. But they make the chopper harder to control if you're making a tight turn.

Like cruisers, choppers usually feature shiny chrome parts. How many a rider adds is limited only by how much he or she wants to spend.

A chopper's front wheel is very thin.

BUILDING A CHOPPER

step 1:

SELECT OR BUILD FRAME: Every chopper starts with a frame. Most choppers use a hard-tail or soft-tail style frame made of steel. Hard-tail frames have no rear suspension. They are simpler to build than soft-tail frames. But the rider usually must endure more bumps and jolts. Before deciding on a frame style, chopper builders must know what other types of parts they want on the bike. For example, frame adjustments need to be made for a very wide rear tire or a very large engine.

step 2:

SELECT AND ADD PARTS: After the frame is finished, builders add the front forks, engine, wheels, and other parts. V-twin engines and polished aluminum wheels are common.

PAINT AND FINISHING TOUCHES: The builder makes sure that the pieces fit together properly. Then pieces are sanded, painted, and polished. Before painting, all surfaces need to be perfectly smooth. From a spiderweb design to a cartoon character, anything goes when it comes to a paint scheme. The possibilities are limited only by the owner's imagination.

TOURING BIKES

If sport bikes are the sprinters of the motorcycle world, then touring bikes are the long-distance runners. It's not unusual for a rider on a touring bike to cover hundreds of miles in one day. Touring bikes offer the plushest, most comfortable ride on two wheels. The best touring bikes give the rider maximum comfort with minimal worries. Popular brands include Harley-Davidson, BMW, Honda, Triumph, and Yamaha.

2006 Honda Gold Wing

2008 Honda Gold Wing

The Honda Gold Wing has been a popular touring bike since it was introduced in 1975. The first model was powered by a 1,000-cc, four-cylinder engine. At that time, it was the biggest Japanese motorcycle.

Today, the Gold Wing remains one of the beefiest bikes around. Some models weigh more than 900 pounds (408 kilograms). It's not always easy to lift it upright so you can start riding. But once you get going, you'll know it was worth the effort. The engine purrs quietly, but gives you fast acceleration.

Options include a satellite-linked navigation system that riders can use to map out their course. Foot-level warm air ducts and a heated seat take the bite out of cold-weather riding. A Gold Wing can even be equipped with an airbag, making it the first production motorcycle with that option. All of these high-tech options, along with sleek styling, put the Gold Wing at the top of the touring class.

Since they're designed for long trips, touring bikes come with a luggage compartment and saddlebags. The luggage compartment is behind the seat. The saddlebags are attached to the sides of the bike. Both the luggage compartment and saddlebags are usually the same color as the rest of the motorcycle.

Tourers are all about plush features. Some of the most common options are cruise control, electronically heated grips and seats, a navigation system, and a modern stereo system with a CD player.

The large fuel tanks usually hold at least 6 gallons (22.7 liters) of fuel. Other bikes usually hold 5 gallons (18.9 liters) or less.

With comfy backrests and roomy seats, touring bikes don't take passengers for granted.

A large front
fairing reduces
wind resistance.

Most tourers have at least
1,200-cc engines.

Cruisers, sport bikes, choppers, and tourers may be the mainstays of the motorcycle world. But they aren't all there is to offer. Some bikes are built just to break records. Others, such as pocket bikes, can be collected as a hobby. Small mopeds fill a basic need by offering reliable yet affordable transportation. And dual-purpose bikes can be ridden on the street or off-road.

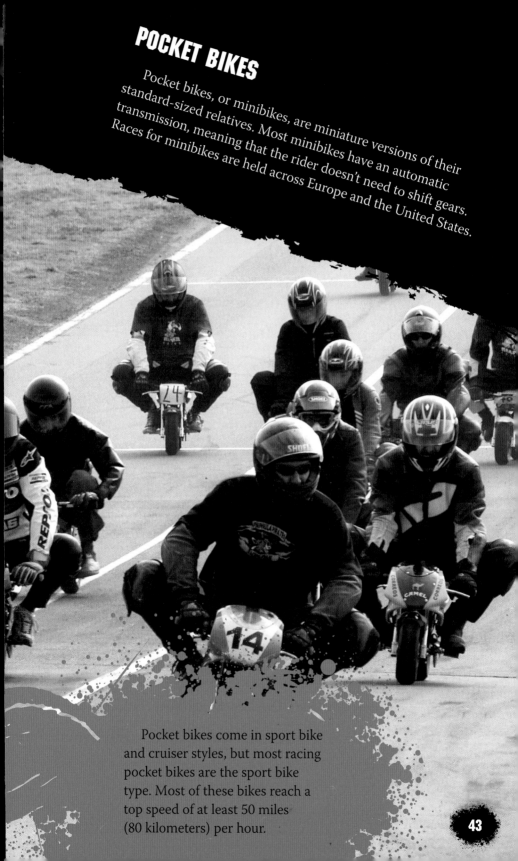

POCKET BIKES

Pocket bikes, or minibikes, are miniature versions of their standard-sized relatives. Most minibikes have an automatic transmission, meaning that the rider doesn't need to shift gears. Races for minibikes are held across Europe and the United States.

Pocket bikes come in sport bike and cruiser styles, but most racing pocket bikes are the sport bike type. Most of these bikes reach a top speed of at least 50 miles (80 kilometers) per hour.

DRAG RACING BIKES

Drag racing bikes speed side by side in a one-on-one fight for the finish line. Cruising down the drag strip, these motorcycles can reach speeds of more than 200 miles (322 kilometers) per hour. The fastest bikes reach the finish line in less than six seconds. Top fuel drag racing bikes use a special type of fuel called nitromethane.

Many drag racers wear helmets that have a built-in helmet sock made of fire-resistant material.

A forward riding position reduces wind resistance.

LAND SPEED BIKES

Land speed bikes are the fastest machines on two wheels. Even the fastest sport bike isn't quick enough to break a land speed record. Many land speed bikes look nothing like standard motorcycles. Some of them are built with a cigar-shaped frame that doesn't even expose the rider to open air.

According to rules set by the Fédération Internationale de Motocyclisme (FIM), a rider's time must break an existing record by at least 1 percent for it to count. Most land speed record-holders achieved their famous feats at the Bonneville Salt Flats in Utah. The fastest land speed bikes can reach speeds of more than 345 miles (555 kilometers) per hour.

A wheelie bar keeps a drag racing bike from popping a wheelie while gaining speed.

GLOSSARY

accelerate (ak-SEH-luh-rayt) — to gain speed

aerodynamic (ayr-oh-dy-NA-mik) — designed to reduce air resistance

chassis (CHA-see) — the main framework of a vehicle to which the other parts are fixed

clearance (KLEER-uhns) — the distance between the ground and the bottom of a motorcycle

cubic centimeter (KYOO-bik SEN-tuh-mee-tuhr) — a unit that measures the size of a motorcycle engine; this unit is abbreviated "cc."

cylinder (SI-luhn-duhr) — a hollow chamber in an engine in which fuel burns to create power

fairing (FAYR-ing) — the outer covering of a motorcycle that protects the rider and helps the bike cut through the air

production (pruh-DUHK-shuhn) — describes a vehicle produced for mass-market sale

transmission (transs-MISH-uhn) — gears that send power from the engine to the rear wheel of a motorcycle; most motorcycles have five or six gears that riders shift through as they accelerate.

tread (TRED) — a series of bumps and deep grooves on a tire

Armentrout, David, and Patricia Armentrout. *Motorcycle Races.* Motorcycle Mania. Vero Beach, Fla.: Rourke, 2008.

Goodman, Susan E. *Motorcycles!* Step into Reading. New York: Random House, 2007.

Graham, Ian. *Motorbikes.* The World's Greatest. Chicago: Raintree, 2006.

Woods, Bob. *Hottest Motorcycles.* Wild Wheels! Berkeley Heights, N.J.: Enslow, 2008.

INTERNET SITES

FactHound offers a safe, fun way to find Internet sites related to this book. All of the sites on FactHound have been researched by our staff.

Here's all you do:

Visit *www.facthound.com*

FactHound will fetch the best sites for you!

INDEX